Protecting the Past

Written by Yvonne Morr
Illustrated by Xiangyi Mo and Jin

My name is Zahra, and I live in Egypt. When I grow up, I would like to be an archaeologist. If I make any important finds, I want them to go to the Egyptian Museum. There everyone will be able to see them. They will also be studied by the world's greatest experts on ancient Egypt.

Contents

Look for the **Thinking Cap**.
When you see this picture, you will find
a problem to think about and write about.

Layla's search

A family tradition

A cloud of hot, dry dust billowed into Layla's face, making her sneeze. She put down her trowel and dusted her hands on her knees. Then she stood up and stretched. Her hands were red and sore, her back ached and the dust had made her throat itch. For the first week of the archaeological dig, Layla had loved every minute, despite the constant aches and pains. But now it was the end of week three, and she had almost nothing to show for her efforts, except a few pieces of a broken pot. She sighed, tucked some loose strands of hair under her scarf and knelt down again. She picked up her brush and began to dust the loose dirt off an ancient wall. But her mind was wandering off.

She was worried. This dig was not going as she had hoped. Why couldn't she find anything important? Other students had. Here she was, a fourth-year university student, in Luxor, Egypt, exploring the ruins of an ancient temple. It was a dream come true. As long as she could remember, she had wanted to be an archaeologist. Layla grew up surrounded by ancient Egyptian culture. Her father was an archaeologist who catalogued objects for the Egyptian Museum in Cairo. Her great-grandfather had been interested in Egypt's treasures too, although not quite in the same way. He had been an **interpreter** on a British treasure-hunting expedition in the 1920s. Both her father and her great-grandfather had been hugely successful in their own ways. Compared to them, she felt like a failure.

interpreter   person who translates aloud for others from one language
to another

Old times, old values

That night after dinner, Layla wandered away from the other students and the professors. They were discussing the temple. Layla would usually have joined in, but tonight she felt too discouraged. She knew that a lot of archaeology involved boring, repetitive work, but she longed for the thrill of discovering something exciting that no one else had seen for thousands of years. How amazing that would feel!

When Layla felt sad, what usually cheered her up was reading from her great-grandfather's diary. It was her most treasured possession, and she took it everywhere she went. She pulled it out now and sat down, opening the dry, old pages at random.

27 April 1928   Luxor

Today was a fine day for treasure! Jones found the ancient robbers' cave that has so long eluded us. The men used a lever to move away the stone slab over the entrance. What riches we found! I have never seen so much gold in one place. Robertson and Jones were so happy, they gave me a sack and let me help myself to some trinkets. There was a solid-gold mask that must be worth a great deal of money, but I was allowed to take only small things. Still, I am very grateful.

Robertson told me that I've done a great job translating for them. I was so happy. The men loaded their camels with sacks of treasure. Robertson and Jones will take the treasure up the Nile, then back to England. I will take my share to Cairo and sell it to the tourists. I will make a fortune!

How different things were back then! Layla knew that if she ever made any interesting finds, she would be allowed to study them, but eventually they would go to the Egyptian Museum. These days, it is illegal to keep any **antiquities**. To think that her great-grandfather had sold his treasures to tourists! Even now his treasures could be in people's living rooms in foreign countries. Layla dreaded thinking about how much Egyptian history had been lost. But, if her great-grandfather hadn't sold all those treasures, her family wouldn't be so well-off now. Thanks to her great-grandfather, they could afford to send Layla to university.

Ancient Egyptian pharaohs were buried with huge fortunes of gold and jewels. As a result, their tombs and pyramids were sought out by robbers from the day they were sealed shut.

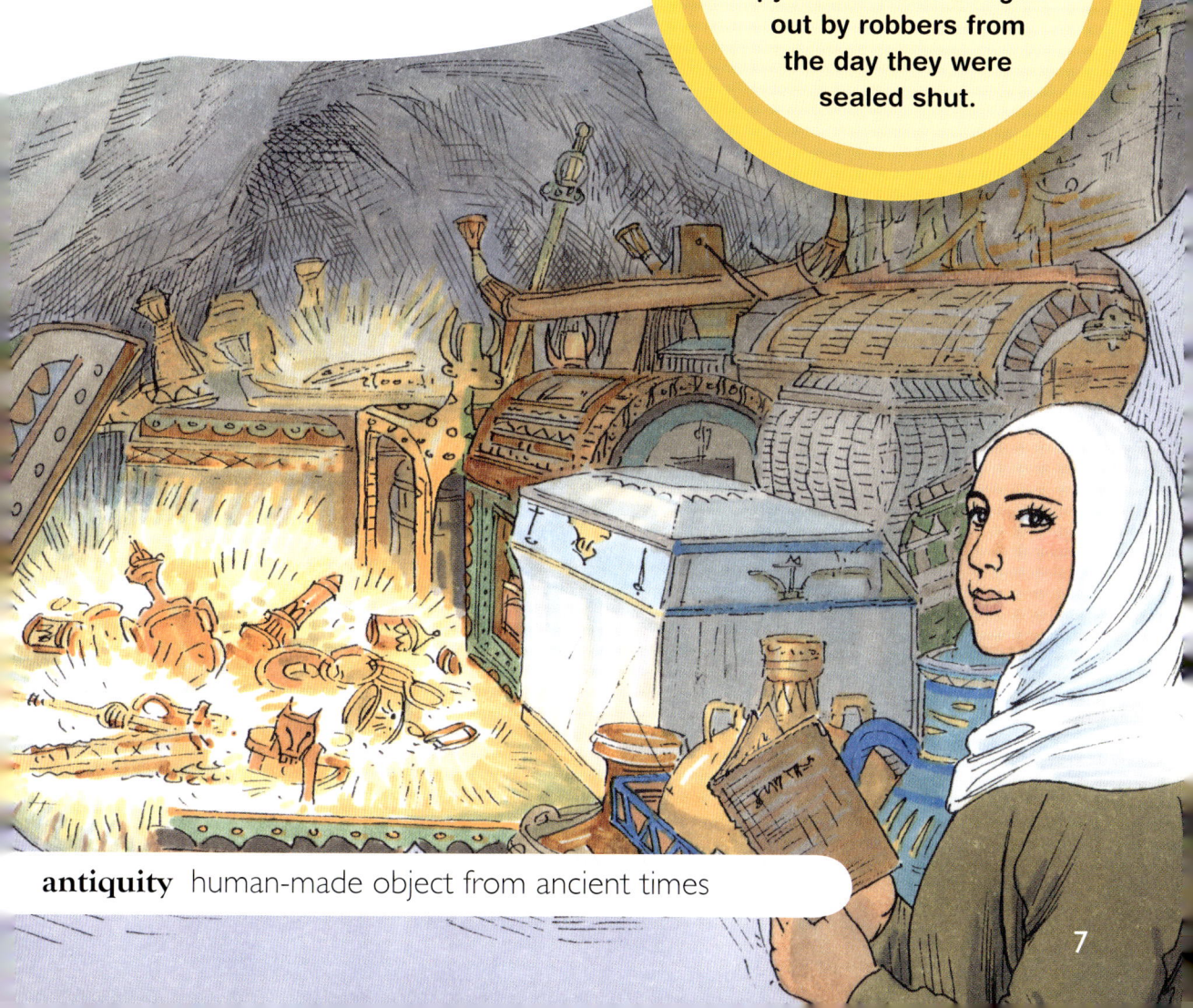

antiquity human-made object from ancient times

The family reunion

The next day, Layla woke up early. Today, her father was arriving in Luxor on a trip to collect **artefacts** for the museum. He was bringing Lateef, Layla's younger brother, with him. Layla's father had promised that they would stop by and see her. Lateef was 11, and a bit of a troublemaker, but Layla adored him. She wished that she'd made a discovery to show her family. Maybe if she made an early start on the dig, she'd get lucky.

By lunchtime, however, she was hot, dusty, thirsty and no better off. As she put down her tools and left the roped-off area, she saw her father and Lateef arriving. Lateef ran over to give her a hug, and then raced away to explore.

'Don't go inside the roped-off area,' Layla called after him, 'and don't touch anything you shouldn't!' Lateef grinned at her, and Layla laughed nervously. Telling Lateef not to do something was a sure way of encouraging him to do it! Layla's father joined her, and the two began talking. Layla forgot to worry about Lateef. It was her first time away from home, and she hadn't seen her father for weeks. She enjoyed catching up on the family news.

Layla's father offered to take her out for lunch, and she agreed eagerly. As she packed up her tools, he went to speak to her professors. She saw Lateef in the distance playing around in the dirt. At least, he wasn't inside the ropes, she thought. 'Time for lunch!' she called to him.

artefact object made by humans long ago

8

Archaeologists must gain permission from landowners before beginning a dig. Then they survey the area, take measurements and make a map. They then divide the site into squares.

Layla's lucky break

They ate at a café on the banks of the Nile. The breeze from the river felt cool and pleasant. Layla chatted with her father about archaeology and the dig. Lateef was bored and started drumming the table with his knife and fork. Layla told her father about her disappointment.

Now Lateef pulled a stone from his pocket and started throwing it high into the air and catching it. He missed a catch, and the stone bounced across the table and onto Layla's plate. Layla frowned. Little brothers! She picked up the stone and put it into her pocket.

After lunch, Layla's father and Lateef waved goodbye, promising to write soon. She grabbed her tools and started walking back to her dig site. She felt the stone in her pocket and pulled it out to throw away.

Something held her back from immediately throwing it. The stone felt a bit odd. She opened her hand and examined it. It was limestone, and one side was flattened. When she wiped it carefully with the corner of her shirt, dirt fell from the cracks. She was amazed to see carvings on the flat side.

Layla's eyes widened. Lateef must have found this near her dig site. Now she couldn't wait to get back there.

History repeats

Back near her dig site, Layla began to search the area where she had seen Lateef crouching before lunch. Four hours later, she knew that she'd found what she was looking for. It was a tall stone pillar, or obelisk, and it was covered with **hieroglyphics**. The obelisk was buried, but one corner was sticking out of the ground. It was this corner that had chipped off. Lateef had picked up the chipped off piece and put it in his pocket. With shaking hands, Layla matched the chip of stone to the corner of the obelisk. It fitted perfectly.

Layla knew at once that this was an important find. It was just outside the roped area, which meant that the temple was bigger than her professors had thought. She ran to tell her professors. The whole team gathered breathlessly around the part of the obelisk that she had uncovered. This was the most exciting find anyone had made on the dig, and it was hers!

hieroglyphics ancient Egyptian writing made up of pictures and symbols

'Well done, Layla,' her professor said. 'This is going to make a great subject for your **thesis**. Not only that, but I want to move some of the team over to this area, and I want you to work with them. Who knows what else we'll find!'

Layla beamed. Now she knew how her great-grandfather must have felt when he saw his riches all those years ago! This time, however, her find would stay in Egypt. Times had changed, she thought, and she was pleased. She wanted her find to be useful for Egypt.

Put on your thinking cap

Write down your thoughts about the following questions. Then discuss them with a classmate.

1. Do you think archaeology is important? Why or why not?

2. How is today's archaeology different from the treasure hunting done by people like Layla's great-grandfather?

3. How do you think Layla feels about what her great-grandfather did with the things he found?

4. Do you think artefacts should be handed over to museums? Why?

thesis long essay describing research about a subject, usually done by university students

What's the issue?

Egypt's riches have always been prized by robbers and treasure hunters. Thousands of years ago, in the time of the pharaohs, the punishment for stealing from a tomb or pyramid was death. In spite of this, many still risked their lives for the chance of instant wealth. Since the time of the ancient Romans, people from other countries have collected Egyptian monuments and smaller artefacts. Some objects were taken illegally, while others were gifts from Egyptian rulers. Many Egyptian artefacts that survive are now in museums and private collections around the world. Unfortunately, even today, precious artefacts are being stolen from Egyptian museums and archaeological sites. The robbers of today are making money by smuggling the culture of Egypt out of the country. Many people are concerned that Egypt is losing its cultural **heritage**.

Many museums around the world have Egyptian antiquities on display. They are often some of the most popular exhibits.

heritage valuable traditions handed down from the past

People are also concerned about objects taken from other places. Thousands of artefacts from ancient sites, such as Angkor Wat in Cambodia and Machu Picchu in Peru, are found in museums all around the world. Many people think that these artefacts should be returned to their countries of origin.

It is only recently that we have come to value old buildings. Many ancient constructions were destroyed in the past by people who used the stone to make their own walls and buildings.

Angkor Wat is a temple complex in Cambodia. It was built in the 1100s. In 2006, an Australian tourist was fined for illegally buying carved stones from the site.

The big five

'Egypt has been deprived of five key items of its cultural heritage. They should be handed back to us,' said Dr Zahi Hawass, of Egypt's Supreme Council of Antiquities. He was speaking at a meeting about the return of cultural property. The five items are located in different countries around the world. They are:

1. The Rosetta Stone in England

2. The Bust of Nefertiti in Germany

3. The Zodiac Ceiling painting from the Dendera Temple in France

4. The statue of Hemiunu, nephew of Pharaoh Khufu, in Germany

5. The Bust of Anchhaf, builder of the Khafre Pyramid, in the United States.

The United Nations will help Egypt to discuss the return of these items with the museums that have them.

The Bust of Nefertiti

Smugglers foiled!

Staff at the Egyptian Museum discovered that the museum had been burgled.

When some archaeologists from Giza asked the museum to return some borrowed objects, the museum staff realised that three statues were missing. They searched through 120,000 objects on display and more than 110,000 objects stored in the basement. But the 4,000-year-old statues were nowhere to be found.

During the investigation, Egypt's Tourism and Antiquities Police received inside information on a smuggling act. Two men were trying to sell the statues by showing photos of them to dealers. Two undercover police pretended to be dealers, and the men were caught.

The thieves had worked for a company that was restoring the museum basement. The men had smuggled the statues out of the building in bags of rubble. They had not been searched at the gates. The museum is now increasing its level of security. From now on, all museum staff will be searched upon leaving the building.

Egyptian museum in Cairo

Theft of precious antiquities is not just a problem in Egypt. Many other museums around the world have strict security to prevent artefacts from being stolen. **Customs officers** in many countries are also alerted to the problem. They confiscate any antiquities that might have been obtained illegally. Many countries are sharing information about stolen objects. They work together to try to catch the thieves.

customs officer official who regulates what things can enter a country

This ancient sculpture was stolen from the Iraq National Museum during the Iraqi war. It has now been returned to the museum.

Write down your thoughts about the following questions. Then discuss them with a classmate.

1. What harm do you think is done by smuggling?

2. There are many poor people living in Egypt. A few of them steal artefacts for money. How do you think they might justify this theft?

3. Do you think every museum employee should be searched every day? Would you feel this way if you worked there?

The Chinese police recovered 8,000 stolen artefacts from northeast China. Some had been illegally excavated, and others had been stolen from museums.

17

Monuments under threat

Many monuments, such as the pyramids of ancient Egypt and the temples of ancient Greece, have stood for thousands of years. Some people think that the monuments will be around forever. However, they may be wrong. Some might be lost within the next 10 years alone.

Antiquities are under threat not only from thieves, but also from well meaning people. For centuries, most Egyptian tombs were sealed-up, dark, dry environments. These conditions were perfect for preserving the things inside, including wall art. Now thousands of tourists visit the tombs, breathing out moist air and touching the walls with greasy fingers. Mould and mildew are starting to grow on the walls, damaging the paint. Outside, the exhaust fumes from tourist buses parked near the monuments damage the rock.

Did you know?

There are two Egyptian obelisks inaccurately known as Cleopatra's Needle. Both obelisks were erected by pharaoh Tuthmosis III in about 1475 BCE (long before the Egyptian pharaoh Cleopatra was born in 69 BCE). One was gifted to England in 1878, and the other was gifted to the United States in 1880.

Even mighty structures such as the temples at the Acropolis in Athens, Greece and the Colosseum in Rome, Italy are not safe. Vibrations from aircraft and traffic are damaging them. Air pollution is creating acid rain, which eats away the rock.

The Cleopatra's Needle given to the United States stands in Central Park, New York. Unfortunately, acid rain and harsh weather are causing the granite to wear away.

Conserving mighty monuments

At the temple complex of Karnak in Egypt (below), visitors might see a worker knocking on the walls and pillars. Upon hearing a hollow ring, the worker injects silicon into holes in the rock, making the structure more stable. This is important conservation work, but sadly many monuments are decaying faster than they can be protected.

The Great Sphinx at Giza (below) is also being restored. In the past, people repaired it with cement and stone that didn't match. These repairs are now being replaced with stone that more closely matches the original.

Cultural heritage around the world

From Machu Picchu to Yale

CUZCO, PERU – In 1911, American Hiram Bingham became the first foreigner to explore the ruins of the ancient Inca city of Machu Picchu. He took about 5,000 artefacts from the site back to Yale University in the United States. Now the Peruvian government wants them all returned. Yale, however, has not done so, saying that Peru would not be able to take care of them properly. Discussions between Yale and the Peruvian government continue.

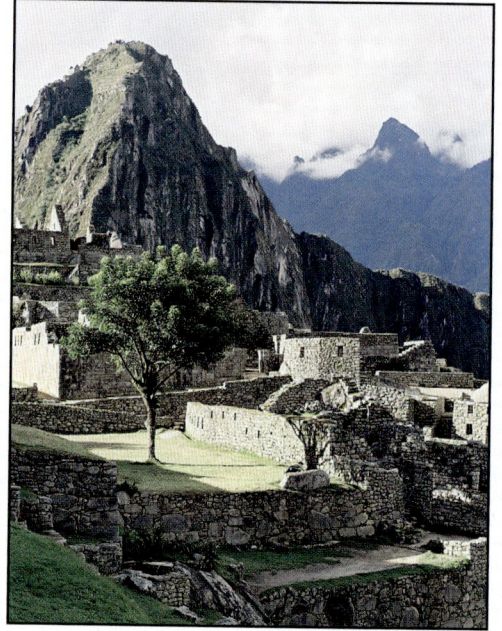

Acid attacks ancient art

WESTERN AUSTRALIA – More than a million carvings detailing the history of Aboriginal people from 6,000 to 30,000 years ago might soon be lost forever. Acid rain from chemical factories in the area has already destroyed about 20 per cent of the carvings. Aboriginal groups are angry about the loss of their carvings. 'It's our culture drawn on those rocks,' a spokesperson said.

Silent subway protest

ATHENS, GREECE – Horses' heads and gods and goddesses stare out of the walls in an Athens subway station. They are replicas of white marble sculptures that once were part of the 2,500-year-old Parthenon Temple. The original sculptures were removed in 1801 and taken to England. The Greeks, however, want them returned.

Museum looted during war

BAGHDAD, IRAQ – Thousands of items have been looted from the Iraq National Museum. In just two days, looters cost Iraq more than 5,500 years of history, worth more than one billion dollars. The looters took mainly valuable items, and it is believed they will be sold to collectors around the world.

Sacred artefacts returned

NEW MEXICO, UNITED STATES – In Albuquerque, eight Native American tribes reclaimed many religious artefacts in a special ceremony. Hundreds of items had been stolen from reservations and sold in the back room of an art gallery.

What's your opinion?

Some ancient artefacts that are housed outside their country of origin were not removed recently. Many ancient obelisks were brought from Egypt to Rome after the Romans conquered Egypt. They have been part of Rome's history for almost 2,000 years. Paris, London and New York have obelisks that were given as gifts by the rulers of Egypt in the 1800s. Many private owners and museums around the world have artefacts that were taken hundreds or even thousands of years ago.

- Should these ancient artefacts be owned by the descendents of the people who found them? Should they belong to the government of the country where they are now, or the government of the country in which they were found? Explain your thoughts.

- Does it make a difference if the artefacts were stolen or given as gifts a long time ago? Why or why not?

- Should people who have paid for artefacts without realising that they were stolen give them up? What would you do if you owned an artefact and found out that it was stolen?

I think artefacts that were stolen should be returned. If people know that stolen artefacts will be taken from them, they will be less likely to buy them. This will stop the looting. However, I think gifts belong to the people they are given to. It is tough luck if you give away things you later decide you want to keep.

Some people think that art belongs to the world. But how would you feel if your stuff was taken without your permission? I think every country should keep the artefacts that are particularly important to it. Less important artefacts could be loaned to museums around the world so that people everywhere can see them.

It's ridiculous to have to return things stolen hundreds of years ago. You can't change history. It is important that we learn about the bad things that have happened in the past so we don't repeat them. Seeing Egyptian obelisks in Rome teaches us about history.

Think tank

1   Does your town or city have any museums? If so, find out which different cultures are represented in the exhibits.

2   Are there any cultural objects in your area that are under threat from the weather or from people's actions? Maybe there is an old building or statue that needs protecting. What can be done to help protect it?

3   Imagine you were digging in your backyard and found something from an ancient civilisation. List the different things you could do with it. What would you decide to do?

Do your own research at the library, on the Internet, or with a parent or teacher to find out about Egypt and learn about how people are trying to preserve its cultural heritage.

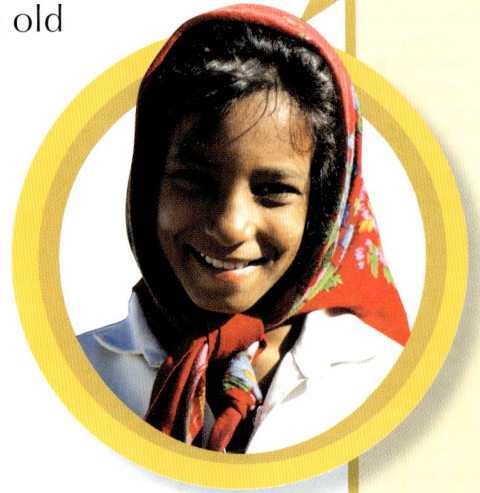

Glossary

antiquity human-made object from ancient times

artefact object made by humans long ago

customs officer official who regulates what things can enter a country

heritage valuable traditions handed down from the past

hieroglyphics ancient Egyptian writing made up of pictures and symbols

interpreter person who translates aloud for others from one language to another

thesis long essay describing research about a subject, usually done by university students